Tattoo

Placement

Theme

Planned Date

Palette

Placement

AF101206

Design

Detail 1

Detail 2

Notes

Tattoo

Placement

Theme

Planned Date

Palette

Placement

Design

Detail 1

Detail 2

Notes

Tattoo

Placement

Theme

Planned Date

Palette

Placement

Design

Detail 1

Detail 2

Notes

Tattoo

Placement

Theme

Planned Date

Palette

Placement

Design

Detail 1

Detail 2

Notes

Tattoo

Placement

Theme

Planned Date

Palette

Placement

Design

Detail 1

Detail 2

Notes

Tattoo

Placement

Theme

Planned Date

Palette

Placement

Design

Detail 1

Detail 2

Notes

Tattoo

Placement

Theme

Planned Date

Palette

Placement

Design

Detail 1

Detail 2

Notes

Tattoo

Placement

Theme

Planned Date

Palette

Placement

Design

Detail 1

Detail 2

Notes

Tattoo

Placement

Theme

Planned Date

Palette

Placement

Design

Detail 1

Detail 2

Notes

Tattoo

Placement

Theme

Planned Date

Palette

Placement

Design

Detail 1

Detail 2

Notes

Tattoo

Placement

Theme

Planned Date

Palette

Placement

Design

Detail 1

Detail 2

Notes

Tattoo

Placement

Theme

Planned Date

Palette

Placement

Design

Detail 1

Detail 2

Notes

Tattoo

Placement

Theme

Planned Date

Palette

Placement

Design

Detail 1

Detail 2

Notes

Tattoo

Placement

Theme

Planned Date

Palette

Placement

Design

Detail 1

Detail 2

Notes

Tattoo

Placement

Theme

Planned Date

Palette

Placement

Design

Detail 1

Detail 2

Notes

Tattoo

Placement

Theme

Planned Date

Palette

Placement

Design

Detail 1

Detail 2

Notes

Tattoo

Placement

Theme

Planned Date

Palette

Placement

Design

Detail 1

Detail 2

Notes

Tattoo

Placement

Theme

Planned Date

Palette

Placement

Design

Detail 1

Detail 2

Notes

Tattoo

Placement

Theme

Planned Date

Palette

Placement

Design

Detail 1

Detail 2

Notes

Tattoo

Placement

Theme

Planned Date

Palette

Placement

Design

Detail 1

Detail 2

Notes

Tattoo

Placement

Theme

Planned Date

Palette

Placement

Design

Detail 1

Detail 2

Notes

Tattoo

Placement

Theme

Planned Date

Palette

Placement

Design

Detail 1

Detail 2

Notes

Tattoo

Placement

Theme

Planned Date

Palette

Placement

Design

Detail 1

Detail 2

Notes

Tattoo

Placement

Theme

Planned Date

Palette

Placement

Design

Detail 1

Detail 2

Notes

Tattoo

Placement

Theme

Planned Date

Palette

Placement

Design

Detail 1

Detail 2

Notes

Tattoo

Placement

Theme

Planned Date

Palette

Placement

Design

Detail 1

Detail 2

Notes

Tattoo

Placement

Theme

Planned Date

Palette

Placement

Design

Detail 1

Detail 2

Notes

Tattoo

Placement

Theme

Planned Date

Palette

Placement

Design

Detail 1

Detail 2

Notes

Tattoo

Placement

Theme

Planned Date

Palette

Placement

Design

Detail 1

Detail 2

Notes

Tattoo

Placement

Theme

Planned Date

Palette

Placement

Design

Detail 1

Detail 2

Notes

Tattoo

Placement

Theme

Planned Date

Palette

Placement

Design

Detail 1

Detail 2

Notes

Tattoo

Placement

Theme

Planned Date

Palette

Placement

Design

Detail 1

Detail 2

Notes

Tattoo

Placement

Theme

Planned Date

Palette

Placement

Design

Detail 1

Detail 2

Notes

Tattoo

Placement

Theme

Planned Date

Palette

Placement

Design

Detail 1

Detail 2

Notes

Tattoo

Placement

Theme

Planned Date

Palette

Placement

Design

Detail 1

Detail 2

Notes

Tattoo

Placement

Theme

Planned Date

Palette

Placement

Design

Detail 1

Detail 2

Notes

Tattoo

Placement

Theme

Planned Date

Palette

Placement

Design

Detail 1

Detail 2

Notes

Tattoo

Placement

Theme

Planned Date

Palette

Placement

Design

Detail 1

Detail 2

Notes

Tattoo

Placement

Theme

Planned Date

Palette

Placement

Design

Detail 1

Detail 2

Notes

Tattoo

Placement

Theme

Planned Date

Palette

Placement

Design

Detail 1

Detail 2

Notes

Tattoo

Placement

Theme

Planned Date

Palette

Placement

Design

Detail 1

Detail 2

Notes

Tattoo

Placement

Theme

Planned Date

Palette

Placement

Design

Detail 1

Detail 2

Notes

Tattoo

Placement

Theme

Planned Date

Palette

Placement

Design

Detail 1

Detail 2

Notes

Tattoo

Placement

Theme

Planned Date

Palette

Placement

Design

Detail 1

Detail 2

Notes

Tattoo

Placement

Theme

Planned Date

Palette

Placement

Design

Detail 1

Detail 2

Notes

Tattoo

Placement

Theme

Planned Date

Palette

Placement

Design

Detail 1

Detail 2

Notes

Tattoo

Placement

Theme

Planned Date

Palette

Placement

Design

Detail 1

Detail 2

Notes

Tattoo

Placement

Theme

Planned Date

Palette

Placement

Design

Detail 1

Detail 2

Notes

Tattoo

Placement

Theme

Planned Date

Palette

Placement

Design

Detail 1

Detail 2

Notes

Tattoo

Placement

Theme

Planned Date

Palette

Placement

Design

Detail 1

Detail 2

Notes

Tattoo

Placement

Theme

Planned Date

Palette

Placement

Design

Detail 1

Detail 2

Notes

Tattoo

Placement

Theme

Planned Date

Palette

Placement

Design

Detail 1

Detail 2

Notes

Tattoo

Placement

Theme

Planned Date

Palette

Placement

Design

Detail 1

Detail 2

Notes

Tattoo

Placement

Theme

Planned Date

Palette

Placement

Design

Detail 1

Detail 2

Notes

Tattoo

Placement

Theme

Planned Date

Palette

Placement

Design

Detail 1

Detail 2

Notes

Tattoo

Placement

Theme

Planned Date

Palette

Placement

Design

Detail 1

Detail 2

Notes

Tattoo

Placement

Theme

Planned Date

Palette

Placement

Design

Detail 1

Detail 2

Notes

Tattoo

Placement

Theme

Planned Date

Palette

Placement

Design

Detail 1

Detail 2

Notes

Tattoo

Placement

Theme

Planned Date

Palette

Placement

Design

Detail 1

Detail 2

Notes

Tattoo

Placement

Theme

Planned Date

Palette

Placement

Design

Detail 1

Detail 2

Notes

Tattoo

Placement

Theme

Planned Date

Palette

Placement

Design

Detail 1

Detail 2

Notes

Tattoo

Placement

Theme

Planned Date

Palette

Placement

Design

Detail 1

Detail 2

Notes

Tattoo

Placement

Theme

Planned Date

Palette

Placement

Design

Detail 1

Detail 2

Notes

Tattoo

Placement

Theme

Planned Date

Palette

Placement

Design

Detail 1

Detail 2

Notes

Tattoo

Placement

Theme

Planned Date

Palette

Placement

Design

Detail 1

Detail 2

Notes

Tattoo

Placement

Theme

Planned Date

Palette

Placement

Design

Detail 1

Detail 2

Notes

Tattoo

Placement

Theme

Planned Date

Palette

Placement

Design

Detail 1

Detail 2

Notes

Tattoo

Placement

Theme

Planned Date

Palette

Placement

Design

Detail 1

Detail 2

Notes

Tattoo

Placement

Theme

Planned Date

Palette

Placement

Design

Detail 1

Detail 2

Notes

Tattoo

Placement

Theme

Planned Date

Palette

Placement

Design

Detail 1

Detail 2

Notes

Tattoo

Placement

Theme

Planned Date

Palette

Placement

Design

Detail 1

Detail 2

Notes

Tattoo

Placement

Theme

Planned Date

Palette

Placement

Design

Detail 1

Detail 2

Notes

Tattoo

Placement

Theme

Planned Date

Palette

Placement

Design

Detail 1

Detail 2

Notes

Tattoo

Placement

Theme

Planned Date

Palette

Placement

Design

Detail 1

Detail 2

Notes

Tattoo

Placement

Theme

Planned Date

Palette

Placement

Design

Detail 1

Detail 2

Notes

Tattoo

Placement

Theme

Planned Date

Palette

Placement

Design

Detail 1

Detail 2

Notes

Tattoo

Placement

Theme

Planned Date

Palette

Placement

Design

Detail 1

Detail 2

Notes

Tattoo

Placement

Theme

Planned Date

Palette

Placement

Design

Detail 1

Detail 2

Notes

Tattoo

Placement

Theme

Planned Date

Palette

Placement

Design

Detail 1

Detail 2

Notes

Tattoo

Placement

Theme

Planned Date

Palette

Placement

Design

Detail 1

Detail 2

Notes

Tattoo

Placement

Theme

Planned Date

Palette

Placement

Design

Detail 1

Detail 2

Notes

Tattoo

Placement

Theme

Planned Date

Palette

Placement

Design

Detail 1

Detail 2

Notes

Tattoo

Placement

Theme

Planned Date

Palette

Placement

Design

Detail 1

Detail 2

Notes

Tattoo

Placement

Theme

Planned Date

Palette

Placement

Design

Detail 1

Detail 2

Notes

Tattoo

Placement

Theme

Planned Date

Palette

Placement

Design

Detail 1

Detail 2

Notes

Tattoo

Placement

Theme

Planned Date

Palette

Placement

Design

Detail 1

Detail 2

Notes

Tattoo

Placement

Theme

Planned Date

Palette

Placement

Design

Detail 1

Detail 2

Notes

Tattoo

Placement

Theme

Planned Date

Palette

Placement

Design

Detail 1

Detail 2

Notes

Tattoo

Placement

Theme

Planned Date

Palette

Placement

Design

Detail 1

Detail 2

Notes

Tattoo

Placement

Theme

Planned Date

Palette

Placement

Design

Detail 1

Detail 2

Notes

Tattoo

Placement

Theme

Planned Date

Palette

Placement

Design

Detail 1

Detail 2

Notes

Tattoo

Placement

Theme

Planned Date

Palette

Placement

Design

Detail 1

Detail 2

Notes

Tattoo

Placement

Theme

Planned Date

Palette

Placement

Design

Detail 1

Detail 2

Notes

Tattoo

Placement

Theme

Planned Date

Palette

Placement

Design

Detail 1

Detail 2

Notes

Tattoo

Placement

Theme

Planned Date

Palette

Placement

Design

Detail 1

Detail 2

Notes

Tattoo

Placement

Theme

Planned Date

Palette

Placement

Design

Detail 1

Detail 2

Notes

Tattoo

Placement

Theme

Planned Date

Palette

Placement

Design

Detail 1

Detail 2

Notes

Tattoo

Placement

Theme

Planned Date

Palette

Placement

Design

Detail 1

Detail 2

Notes

Tattoo

Placement

Theme

Planned Date

Palette

Placement

Design

Detail 1

Detail 2

Notes

Tattoo

Placement

Theme

Planned Date

Palette

Placement

Design

Detail 1

Detail 2

Notes

Tattoo

Placement

Theme

Planned Date

Palette

Placement

Design

Detail 1

Detail 2

Notes

Tattoo

Placement

Theme

Planned Date

Palette

Placement

Design

Detail 1

Detail 2

Notes

Tattoo

Placement

Theme

Planned Date

Palette

Placement

Design

Detail 1

Detail 2

Notes

Tattoo

Placement

Theme

Planned Date

Palette

Placement

Design

Detail 1

Detail 2

Notes

Tattoo

Placement

Theme

Planned Date

Palette

Placement

Design

Detail 1

Detail 2

Notes

Tattoo

Placement

Theme

Planned Date

Palette

Placement

Design

Detail 1

Detail 2

Notes

Tattoo

Placement

Theme

Planned Date

Palette

Placement

Design

Detail 1

Detail 2

Notes

Tattoo

Placement

Theme

Planned Date

Palette

Placement

Design

Detail 1

Detail 2

Notes

Tattoo

Placement

Theme

Planned Date

Palette

Placement

Design

Detail 1

Detail 2

Notes

Tattoo

Placement

Theme

Planned Date

Palette

Placement

Design

Detail 1

Detail 2

Notes

Tattoo

Placement

Theme

Planned Date

Palette

Placement

Design

Detail 1

Detail 2

Notes

Tattoo

Placement

Theme

Planned Date

Palette

Placement

Design

Detail 1

Detail 2

Notes

Tattoo

Placement

Theme

Planned Date

Palette

Placement

Design

Detail 1

Detail 2

Notes

Tattoo

Placement

Theme

Planned Date

Palette

Placement

Design

Detail 1

Detail 2

Notes

Tattoo

Placement

Theme

Planned Date

Palette

Placement

Design

Detail 1

Detail 2

Notes

Tattoo

Placement

Theme

Planned Date

Palette

Placement

Design

Detail 1

Detail 2

Notes

Tattoo

Placement

Theme

Planned Date

Palette

Placement

Design

Detail 1

Detail 2

Notes

Tattoo

Placement

Theme

Planned Date

Palette

Placement

Design

Detail 1

Detail 2

Notes

Tattoo

Placement

Theme

Planned Date

Palette

Placement

Design

Detail 1

Detail 2

Notes

Tattoo

Placement

Theme

Planned Date

Palette

Placement

Design

Detail 1

Detail 2

Notes

www.ingramcontent.com/pod-product-compliance
Lightning Source LLC
LaVergne TN
LVHW012117070526
838202LV00056B/5761